Little Mitchie

WACKY INVENTIONS

WEIRD, WILD, AND WONDERFUL

TAMRA B. ORR

CREATING YOUNG NONFICTION READERS

Little Mitchie books spark curiosity and support early nonfiction reading for students in Grades 2-3. Designed to build vocabulary, support second language learners, and prepare readers for middle-grade content, each book includes helpful tips for parents and educators to build confidence and deepen understanding of the world.

TIPS FOR READING NONFICTION WITH BEGINNING READERS

Talk about Nonfiction

Begin by explaining that nonfiction books give us information that is true. The book will be organized around a specific topic or idea, and we may learn new facts through reading.

Look at the Parts

Most nonfiction books have helpful features. Our *Little Mitchie* titles include color photographs and graphic aids, a table of contents, a glossary, and an index. Share the purpose of these features with your reader.

Color Photos and Graphic Aids

A lot of information can be found by "reading" photos, charts, maps, and other graphic aids found within nonfiction texts. Help your reader learn more about the different ways information can be displayed.

Table of Contents

Located at the front of the book, this list shows the big ideas within the text and the page numbers where they can be found.

Glossary

Located at the back of the book, the glossary defines key words and phrases that are related to the topic. These words and phrases can be found in the text in colored type.

Index

Located at the back of the book, an index is an alphabetical list of topics and the page numbers where they can be found.

With a little help and guidance about reading nonfiction, you can feel good about introducing a young reader to the world of *Little Mitchie* nonfiction books.

Little Mitchie is an imprint of:

Mitchell Lane
PUBLISHERS

2001 SW 31st Avenue
Hallandale, FL 33009
mitchelllanepub.com

First Edition, 2027.

Author: Tamra B. Orr
Designer: Jen Bowers
Editor: Tricia Hoffman

Library of Congress Cataloging-in-Publication Data
Title: Wacky Inventions / by Tamra Orr

Description: Hallandale, FL :
Mitchell Lane Publishers, [2027]

Identifiers:
ISBN 979-8-89260-895-4 (library bound)
ISBN 979-8-89260-998-2 (eBook)

Library of Congress Control Number: 2026936372

PHOTO CREDITS
Shutterstock: cover, p.1 ©2019 Duntrune Studios, p.5 ©2018 vk_st, ©2015 Everett Collection, p.7 CC BY 4.0 Erik Holmén/Nordiska museet, ©2022 ian goodridge, p.8–9, 18 Public Domain/Rare Historical Photos, ©2022 Here, p.10 CC BY-SA 3.0/Zenit, p.11 Public Domain/U.S. Army Images, p.12 Public Domain/Rare Historical Photos, p.13 ©2017 Cast Of Thousands, p.14 ©2015 Littlekidmoment, Evans/Three Lions/Hulton Archive/Getty Images, p.15 ©2019 Duntrune Studios, p.17 ©2017 Ground Picture, p.18 ©2025 Shawn.ccf, p.19 ©2020 Marut Sayannikroth, p.20 ©2015 kdshutterman, p.21 ©2024 Dmitriy Fesenko, p.22 Public Domain/Rare Historical Photos, Geeky Gadgets

TABLE OF CONTENTS

Chapter One

WACKY CREATIONS

Throughout history, inventors have had exciting ideas and made them real. Some of these inventions made life easier. Some made life more fun. And some were just wacky!

INCREDIBLE INVENTOR

Thomas Edison is one of the most important inventors in history. He invented the first modern light bulb, the **phonograph**, and the motion picture camera.

Chapter Two

FROM HERE TO THERE

Bicycles were first invented in 1817. But in the late 1800s, some inventors created a hydrocycle. It was a bicycle crossed with a boat for taking rides on water.

A FASTER RIDE

In Germany in the 1930s, rocket-powered bikes could go 50 miles (80 km) per hour. Today, similar bicycles are still made. They can hit more than 200 miles (322 km) per hour!

Inventor J.H. Purves created the Dynasphere in 1930. Known as "Jumbo," it was just one big wheel! One or two passengers could ride inside it.

MEET THE TURTLE

In 1775, a wooden ball called the Turtle was invented. It traveled underwater using hand cranks and foot pedals. It was used to attach explosives to the **hulls** of enemy ships!

In the mid-1950s, a helicopter company invented the Aerocycle. Pilots stood on a platform with powerful **rotating** blades right below them. The Aerocycle could reach 75 miles (120 km) per hour and could stay in the air for 45 minutes!

Chapter Three

AN EASIER LIFE?

Inventors are always trying to find ways to make life easier. In 1939, people were tired of winter weather. So, inventors in Montreal, Canada, created the blizzard cone. It was a long, pointy plastic face shield to protect against snow and ice.

ZAP THAT FRECKLE

Don't try this at home! An Italian doctor found a way to remove pesky freckles. Using **carbon dioxide** in the form of dry ice, he would freeze the skin. When the skin healed, the freckle was gone. It might have worked, but it really hurt!

Do you struggle to eat spaghetti? You're not alone. In the 1970s, an **engineer** designed a fork that could twirl those slippery noodles with the push of a button. Today, you can buy a battery-powered version.

NO FEEDING NEEDED

A pet is a big responsibility. In 1975, one man invented an easy one: the pet rock. It was a rock with googly eyes, a name, and a 32-page manual on how to care for it. Millions of people bought them!

Chapter Four

TODAY'S INVENTIONS

Today's inventors have new ideas that are both incredible—and incredibly wacky! For example, the selfie stick. First invented in Japan in the 1980s, it keeps being updated. Hundreds of thousands have been sold around the world.

Be You

A Japanese company has invented a new "human washing machine" that's not made for clothes! Climb in, close the lid, and get a wash and rinse. In this special machine designed just for people, you'll be fully clean in 15 minutes.

USELESS ON PURPOSE

In Japan, there is a word for inventions that are useless on purpose: *chindogu*. Examples include an umbrella for your camera, a broom and dust pan attachment for your slippers, and a toilet paper hat.

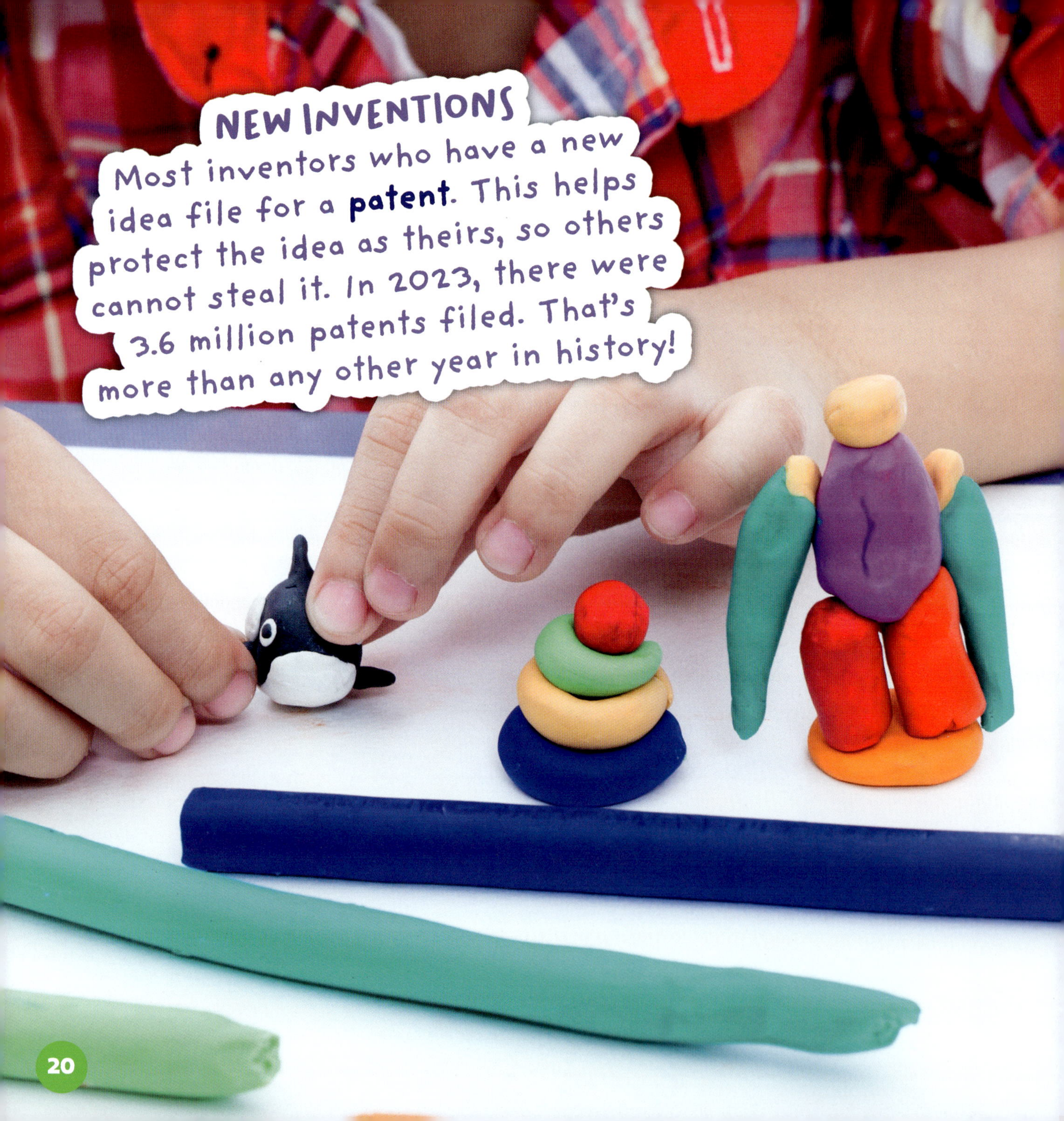

NEW INVENTIONS

Most inventors who have a new idea file for a **patent**. This helps protect the idea as theirs, so others cannot steal it. In 2023, there were 3.6 million patents filed. That's more than any other year in history!

Sometimes an invention works better for something completely different from what was intended. Play-doh® was originally made to clean wallpaper. The Slinky® was supposed to be a spring to use on huge ships. What wacky invention might be next?

EVEN WILDER!

Reading in bed can be uncomfortable. So, in the 1930s, people wore Hamblin glasses. They used mirrors so readers could see a book at the perfect angle.

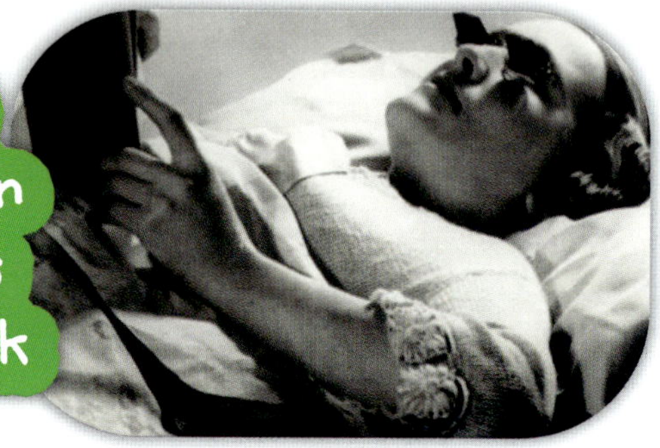

In Japan in the 1960s, people tried the Cat-Mew Machine to get rid of mice. It meowed every 10 minutes to hopefully scare away rodents. (Spoiler: it didn't!)

Searching for treasure? Try metal-detecting sandals. As you walk, they scan for valuables!

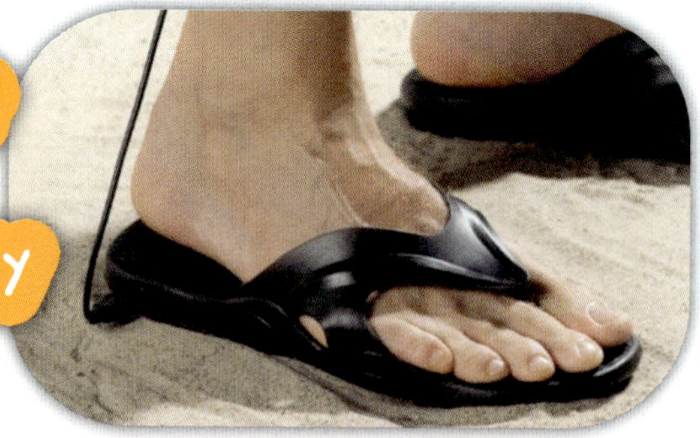

GLOSSARY

carbon dioxide (kahr-buhn dye-ahk-side) a colorless, odorless gas

engineer (en-juh-neer) someone who is specially trained to design and build machines

hulls (huhlz) the frame or body of a boat or ship

patent (pat-uhnt) a legal document giving the inventor of an item the sole rights to make and sell it

phonograph (foh-nuh-graf) a machine that picks up and reproduces the sounds that have been recorded in the grooves cut into a record

rodents (roh-duhnts) mammals, such as mice, rats, and beavers, that have large, sharp front teeth used for gnawing

rotating (roh-tay-ting) moving in a circle around a central point

FURTHER READING

Keppeler, Jill. *Weird Food Inventions.* Gareth Stevens Publishing, 2019.

Murphy, Jim. *Weird & Wacky Inventions.* Sky Pony, 2016.

ON THE INTERNET

15 Of the Coolest Accidental Inventions
https://science.howstuffworks.com/innovation/inventions/15-of-the-coolest-accidental-inventions.htm
How Stuff Works explains 15 accidental inventions, from super glue to popsicles.

20 Weird Inventions The World Just Wasn't Prepared For
www.boredpanda.com/random-weird-inventions/#_
Take a look at 20 weird inventions, including a selfie toaster and a portable radio hat.

INDEX